Intimate Bedfellows:

Love, Sex, and the Catholic Church

Intimate Bedfellows:
Love, Sex, and the Catholic Church

by Thomas and Donna Finn

Illustrated by Chris Ware

St. Paul Books & Media

Nihil Obstat:
    Very Rev. Timothy J. Shea, V.F.

Imprimatur:
    + Bernard Cardinal Law
    November 20, 1992

Library of Congress Cataloging-in-Publication Data

Finn, Thomas.
    Intimate bedfellows : love, sex, and the Catholic Church / by
Thomas Finn and Donna Finn.
        p.   cm.
    Includes bibliographical references.
    ISBN 0-8198-3667-2
    1. Sex—Religious aspects—Catholic Church.   2. Sexual ethics.
3. Catholic Church—Doctrines.   I. Finn, Donna.   II. Title.
BX1795.S48F56   1993
241'.66—dc20   92-42622
                                                                          CIP

Appendix A reprinted with permission from *Love and Relationships: God's Plan for Human Sexuality*. Thomas and Donna Finn. Copyright 1991. Hi-Time Publishing Corp.

Cover design and illustrations by Chris Ware.

Printed and published in the U.S.A. by St. Paul Books & Media,
50 St. Paul's Ave., Boston, MA 02130

St. Paul Books & Media is the publishing house of the Daughters of St. Paul, an international congregation of women religious serving the Church with the communications media.

         1 2   3 4 5 6 7   8 9   99 98 97   96 95 94 93

Contents

Foreword

Although it is true that the teaching of the Catholic Church on moral matters has been appreciated and followed faithfully over the centuries, it is also true that within particular cultures and times various elements of that teaching have met with skepticism, rejection and even ridicule. The last thirty years have witnessed both acceptance and rejection with regard to particular aspects of the Church's teaching on marriage and human sexuality. Doubtless, its teaching on contraception has been the focus of great controversy.

This booklet expresses the reflections of a couple concerning their own journey towards an appreciation of that teaching. In recounting their experience, the authors disclose to the reader their profound reverence for the meanings and purposes of human sexuality, and for the wisdom and love of God reflected in them.

The authors share with the reader many insights regarding the bond of marriage, the significance of marital fidelity, and the inherent values of human procreation. The authors also offer an evaluation of certain actions that violate these goods of marriage. Among those evaluated are: pre-marital and extra-marital sexual intercourse, cohabitation, contraception and sterilization. These discussions demonstrate a true appreciation not only of the Church's teaching on these matters, but also of the reasons supporting this teaching.

In their discussion of "responsible parenthood" the authors provide a valuable service to all couples who have difficulty understanding the moral difference between contraception and natural family planning. This discussion does not attempt to engage all of the philosophical and theological argumentation put forward in academic texts, but speaks from the experience of a couple whose marriage has grown and developed through the use of natural family planning. Many couples will find encouragement in the authors' testimony regarding the effectiveness of natural family planning methods in spacing births, and about its growth-promoting and marriage-enriching dimensions.

Intimate Bedfellows... provides valuable testimony and helpful explanations to all who desire a better appreciation of the Church's teaching on marriage and human sexuality.

Rev. Kevin T. McMahon, STD
Professor of Moral Theology
St. Charles Borromeo Seminary
Overbrook, Pennsylvania

Acknowledgments

To all those who have helped us in the writing of *Intimate Bedfellows: Love, Sex, and the Catholic Church,* we offer our sincere thanks. Especially to Mother Shaun Vergauwen, FSE, and Sr. Barbara Johnson, FSE, of the Franciscan Life Center in Meriden, CT; Louise Pyers, editor of *Family Seasons Magazine*; Stephen and Rosemary Kern, coordinators of Natural Family Planning in the Diocese of Metuchen, NJ; Rev. Robert Tucker, director of vocations in the Archdiocese of Hartford; Chris and Don Paglia, co-directors of the Family Life Office for the Archdiocese of Hartford; Rev. Kevin T. McMahon, STD, of St. Charles Borromeo Seminary; and to our editor, Sr. Theresa Frances, FSP. Your input and ideas were invaluable, your support and encouragement were life-giving.

Introduction

Check out the popular Saturday morning TV shows enjoyed by kids today and you will find that most of them present the adventures of some hero or another. The heroes of many kids today are Teenage Mutant Ninja Turtles, Batman, Transformers, and scores of others. These cartoon characters truly capture a child's imagination, and, on some level, they give children a taste of right vs. wrong.

In the 1960's, when Saturday morning television was a big deal for us, one of our favorite characters was the Lone Ranger. Wearing a mask and dressed in clean shiny clothes, we can remember watching this cowboy

hero do all sorts of "good guy" things. We'd watch him catch bad guys (dressed in dark, dirty clothes, of course), right wrongs and protect the helpless. And he always left behind a silver bullet as a symbol of his honesty and moral virtue. Let's face it, this guy knew right from wrong.

If we survey today's "moral landscape" in the area of sexuality, it seems evident that an intense struggle exists in the search for moral truths. In fact, with the exception of crimes such as rape and child abuse, our society seems not to have any clearly defined sexual values. This struggle takes on a personal dimension as we try to define our own values in the area of sexuality. Over the course of our engagement and marriage, we have faced varying degrees of confusion in regard to the moral questions inherent in our love relationship. Frankly, we often would have been thrilled if someone had rode a horse onto our front lawn and said, "Howdy, pardners, I'm the Love Ranger, and here's the right thing to do." So far, however, he's been a no-show, and the struggle moves on.

For us as Christians, however, we do have moral guidelines given to us by Jesus and taught by his Church. In our Roman Catholic tradition, there exists a rich body of wisdom in the area of human sexuality which stands out clearly in the sea of gray. Much of this teaching has been newly expressed in recent years by Pope Paul VI and Pope John Paul II in ways which are spiritually inspiring. But the interpretation and integration of these teachings into the mainstream of marriage and relationships is not always easy.

At the end of the Lone Ranger show, someone always asked, "Who was that masked man?" In this question was an acknowledgment that, although people knew the Lone Ranger stood for goodness and truth, there was a certain mystery about him. For many of us, our experience of the Catholic Church in the area of sexual values is not so different. We believe that the Church promotes goodness and truth, but the teachings in the area of sexual morality seem to be masked in mystery.

Whether you are engaged, married or simply looking for greater understanding in the area of human sexuality, we invite you to read on in a spirit of openness. None of what follows is intended to be judgmental in any way. Rather, *Intimate Bedfellows...* is meant to be a brief summary of our experiences with love, sex, and marriage within the Church. We hope this can be helpful in your ongoing journey of human love. We believe that the Church's teachings have received a biased presentation with an over-emphasis on the moralistic "Don't do this" aspects of it. We would like these pages to reflect the joyful, loving, relationship-building side of the Catholic Church's teachings on human sexuality and marriage.

1
The Question of Conscience

Do This vs. Don't Do That

Before beginning any discussion of specific Church teachings, it is important that we have an understanding of human conscience. Through our teens and twenties, we frankly had a hard time understanding what "conscience" really was. We often found ourselves having a difficult time balancing mixed messages of "follow the voice of your conscience," and "this is what you should do." Sometimes we felt stuck in a "Do this" vs. "Don't do that" debate. It was like the old cartoon segments which portray an angel and a devil perched on opposite shoul-

ders of the character, each trying to persuade the character to "go my way."

After we had dated for two years, Donna moved into her first apartment. When we would get together for weekend visits, we now faced the decision: Do we stay overnight in the apartment, or does Tom do the motel scene? We felt caught in between society's and many of our friends' positions which said, "What's the big deal? Stay together." And our parents and Church's position which said, "Look, this *is* a big deal. Consider other arrangements." The voices of "Do this, vs. Don't do that" were very strong. And our decision to not stay together led to finding a local family who was willing to let Tom sleep at their house. That decision was the right one for us, and, looking back, it strengthened our sense of responsibility for our own choices.

We can begin our exploration of conscience by seeing the Church and secular society as sitting opposite one another on our shoulders, each trying to influence our moral values. Perhaps many of us would like to switch off this debate, yet God challenges us to seek his truth and to make our moral decisions accordingly. The key to our understanding of this question of conscience is in the words "right conscience" and "objective norms of morality," vs. "purely subjective conscience" and "personal opinion."

When it comes to matters of conscience, we cannot rely on a "purely subjective conscience." A purely subjective conscience is, basically, personal opinion, or what seems right or most comfortable in any given situation. Instead, our responsibility is to develop a right conscience, or, a correctly "informed conscience"—one which we can rely upon to guide us in making correct decisions. That requires a clear understanding of issues and a mature understanding of what God has revealed to be true—

the truths which God has revealed are "the objective norms of morality."

In the 1960's the Second Vatican Council gave a beautiful definition to conscience when it said: "In the depths of his conscience, man detects a law which he does not impose upon himself, but which holds him to obedience. Always summoning him to love good and avoid evil, the voice of conscience when necessary speaks to his heart: do this, shun that. For man has in his heart a law written by God; to obey it is the very dignity of man.... Hence, the more right conscience holds sway, the more persons and groups turn aside from blind choice and strive to be guided by the objective norms of morality."[1]

For us, it helps to read that over a few times for it to sink in, especially the part about God's law speaking to our heart. Too often our society equates the phrase "Follow your heart" with "If it feels good, do it." But this is not the essence of conscience. To have a law of God written in our heart means that he created us to live in accordance with certain values which he knew would be best for us.

When we are faced with a moral decision then, it is possible for us to know that law—to hear that voice—deep in our hearts calling us to "do this; shun that." Society's voice might tell us instead, "Hey, what you hear is only guilt feelings left over from rigid, puritanical ways of looking at things. C'mon, friend, do your own thing, truth is subjective." That voice speaking to our heart, however, is objective truth, God's truth, and God wants us to do all we can to hear him and move toward a correctly informed conscience.

If we only rely on a subjective conscience to guide our decisions, we can sometimes put ourselves in a position similar to buying an appliance in one of those low priced, no money down, $11.00 a month come-on deals. On the surface, it looks like a great value, but on further analysis it proves to be an inferior product. After the finance charges are added up, the "bargain" item costs more than a better model paid for at the time of purchase. In other words, without a full study of all the issues and factors involved, what seems at first glance to be best (the personal opinion, or the "socially acceptable" choice) isn't always the best option. The correct, "informed" choice, on the other hand, takes into account all aspects of an issue, present and future. It is the choice which—while perhaps being immediately more difficult—reaps the most benefit over the long run.

Sexual Behavior and Conscience

The above example also applies to matters of conscience in the area of sexual behavior. It is easy to confuse conscience with personal opinion, based on what seems "right for me" in any given situation. After several decades of exposure to self-centered and secular principles, it is difficult to accept that what seems right for me may not be the morally correct choice. Part of this is due to the discomfort we naturally feel when told what to do in our personal lives. Many single adults, married couples and teenagers feel resentment toward persons or institutions (such as the Church) whom they see as attempting to control their sexual behavior. But in considering the issue of conscience, we ask you to be open to the question "What does God think is best?" "Is this act good in itself?" "Is it good for me to do this at this particular moment?" "Do I have the right intention in doing this?"

Indeed, what the Church asks of us is to make decisions concerning issues like pre-marital sex, cohabitation and contraception in a context greater than personal opinion, or of what seems personally right for you and your spouse or fiancee, your boyfriend or girlfriend. Our goal becomes the development of a truly informed conscience, one which understands that decisions regarding sexual morality involve responsibilities toward ourselves, our partner *and* God. Such a correctly informed conscience requires the awareness that sexual activity reaches the profound psycho-sexual levels of human experience wherein we are in touch with the deeper meaning of life, where God is intimately present to us.

An informed conscience is one which understands that the way we treat one another sexually has a lasting impact on our innermost sense of who we are. It is one which is open to pursuing the knowledge of a true right and a true wrong. It starts with an open question, and seeks information on all sides of the subject—not as a means of confirming one's bias or defensively held opinion, but rather as a means of determining the truth concerning the issue at hand, much like a courtroom jury is called upon to do.

Conscience and Free Will

The notion of objective truth also comes into play when we talk about free will. God has created us with free will and desires that we use it, but free will is not license to do as we please. With the exercise of free will we must accept responsibility for seeking the truth—in this case, the truth about sexual issues—in an honest, open fashion and then try to live our lives accordingly. This search for truth includes an understanding of our nature as sexual beings. The fact that God has a plan for us, by which he wants us to attain the fullness of life, can be difficult to accept and understand. It is in direct contrast to the secular humanist philosophy that truth is determined by a person's own experience of life. It is as

if a gang of angels had written on a playground wall, "*God Rules*," and then a gang of humans came along and wrote, "*People Rule*." We watch this happen over and over, and we can't help but wonder who's right.

Our decisions regarding sexual values and actions are not the same type of decision as what to order for dinner, or which pair of shoes to wear. They are not to be made according to someone else's opinion or society's current standards. Rather, we are challenged to make our decisions on moral issues based on the truth of God's design for love, marriage and sexual intimacy.

Summary

We are called to share fully in God's plan for creation. It is by living in a close, cooperative relationship with God, our Creator, that we can experience the fullness of life. That kind of a relationship requires our looking honestly at what God intends our relationship with him and others to be and then basing our choices on that knowledge. By choosing what we understand to be God's desires, we move closer to him; by choosing other than what he desires, we move away from him. Ultimately, these choices involve you, your partner and God. Keep these ideas of objective truth and informed conscience on a front burner as you continue reading. They can be helpful in obtaining a broader picture of the Church's teachings on sexuality.

2
Pre-Marital Sex

Looking for the Big Picture

Most of us have heard somewhere along the way about the Catholic Church's teaching that sexual intercourse is to be reserved for marriage. The question is, "Why?" Why should we choose to hold ourselves back from something so enjoyable, powerful and sensual until after the wedding ceremony? Questions such as these are best answered by looking beyond the "reserve for marriage" sign and discovering what a Christian understanding of marriage actually entails. We can start by looking at some of society's methods of assessing "readiness" for important or significant responsibilities.

Can you recall learning to drive? As a rule, we cannot legally drive until we have met a number of requirements set by civil law. When we are thirteen, even though we may "know" how to drive, why can't we ask Mom and Dad for the keys and drive off? The practical answers are, of course, that we could be arrested, our parents could be dropped from their insurance company or be sued or fined if we hurt anyone in an accident. The broader answer is that certain standards are required to help assure some degree of stability and safety in our society. We have to be a certain age, able to read and understand basic symbols, pass tests which assess our understanding of the rules of the roads, and demonstrate our competence behind the wheel before we can put a driver's license in our pockets. Drinking ages, for example, are set regardless of one's personal ability to tolerate alcohol and drink responsibly. Military service is possible only after reaching a certain age and successfully completing basic training, regardless of one's desire to serve. Scholastic degrees are awarded only after a course of studies is completed and one's competence has been demonstrated, regardless of a student's desire for the degree.

Some Things Are Important

What does all this have to do with sexual behavior? Basically, laws such as these are one of society's ways of saying that certain things "mean" something. They are statements that some things are important and are not routine. They indicate that our physical or emotional maturing, our efforts, our knowledge, and our experience reflect a certain degree of growth and maturity. The specific event which signifies the success of one's efforts—the driver's license, the passed exam or the graduation—affirms a person's past development and represents a readiness to move on to new and deeper levels of growth, experience and service. The Church teaches that sexual intimacy is to be reserved for marriage because intercourse "means" something quite special. Sexual intercourse represents the deepest level of intimacy and self-giving that two people can share. In fact, sexual intercourse serves as a sign to one another that we are committed forever to the vows of our marriage.

We admit, obviously, that Church teaching is quite different from laws regulating driver's licenses and drinking ages. The latter are man-made, while the Church's teaching is based on what is called "natural" or "moral" law. The difference is critical so, once again, let's think this through.

Recall in our discussion about conscience that we spoke about a law written in our hearts which holds the voice of God calling us to do what is right and avoid what is wrong. This law is not man-made or arbitrary, rather it reflects deep, unchanging and fundamental principles which can be known by everyone.

These "natural" or "moral" laws grow from the very essence of what it means to be a human being and reflect the dignity that you and I possess by virtue of our being human persons. In other words, we are people of infinite, immeasurable worth and value because we are created by God. Since he created us, there must be certain moral principles he intended us to live by which are written into the owner's manual of our hearts. In this "manual" exists the instructions on how God "means things to be" when it comes to matters of morality.

The Church, then, doesn't make these laws up— that is, they are not man-made, God made them. Instead, the Church proclaims these moral laws with the intention of helping us to better live the life God wants us to live. In a sense, the Church's role is to help us understand our own God-given owner's manual, and, in doing so, helps to protect and enrich our basic human dignity and worth. This is especially true in matters of marriage and family life where the natural laws underlying "reserve sex for marriage" take root.

Sexual Intercourse: The Ultimate Sign

The Church does not see your wedding day as an end point, but as a moving into deeper levels of growth, experience and service to one another. From the time that you start dating casually, to serious dating, to being engaged, you are developing many facets of your relationship simply through the time and effort you give in getting to know and love each other. It is in these deeper levels of relationship that sexual intimacy finds its true meaning. What is this meaning? The answer can be understood by looking at what God intends sexual intercourse to be.

We were created to live in a mutually loving relationship with our Creator. Along the way, however, people managed to fall rather far away from the path toward God and became involved in sinful, self-centered, alienating activities. God sent his only Son, Jesus, to be our Savior, to live among us. As a human being, Jesus showed us how to live in a loving relationship with the Father. Jesus' gift to us is love; as the greatest sign of his love, Jesus gave his body through his suffering and death on the cross. It was the ultimate, most personal, most powerful way in which he could demonstrate his love for us and for the Father. In a sense then, Jesus' death—the giving of his body—was sacramental. His life and death signified God's committed, unconditional and undying love for us.

The ultimate, most personal and powerful sign of a husband and wife's love for each other is normally expressed in the intimacy of sexual intercourse. The Church holds that in this intimate way, God's love for us takes on human expression (cf Eph 5:21-32). Just as a man and a woman give their bodies to one another as a sign of the depth of their love and respect for each other, so Jesus gave his body to show us the depth of his love.[2] Sexual intercourse is our most intimate way of expressing to one another our faithful love—a love which is both unitive and life-giving. By unitive and life-giving we mean that it strengthens the exclusive love of our marriage, reaffirms our permanent commitment, and brings into ever greater focus the gift that we are to one another.

This unitive and life-giving meaning of intercourse is a reflection of the principles which are basic to the sacrament of marriage. If we take a look at the traditional marriage rite we will see that there are three principles or qualities of marriage that we commit to through the old "I do."

These three principles are:

1. That our marriage will be "unitive." In promising this, sexual intercourse will be an expression or sign of our unity to be nurtured in daily self-giving and sharing of life's hopes, joys and sorrows.

2. That our marriage will be "fruitful." Here, we promise that our marriage and our sharing of intercourse will be open to new life and be a true sharing in the creative work of God. (More on this in a later chapter.)

3. That our marriage commitment will endure for our lifetime. Our promise to each other, God, and to those present is to give ourselves totally, unconditionally and forever to this person we're marrying.

In the total self-giving of sexual intercourse, then, there is no room for thoughts of "today, but not forever," or, "I'll try it out first, then I'll decide...."

We hope that you can see now why pre-marital sex is not reflective of such a fully committed, fruitful and unitive love between a man and a woman. Nor does it signify God's total and everlasting love for us. To be redemptive, Jesus' actions had to reflect the meaning God intended them to have. His actions were a true reflection of God's fully committed, unconditional and undying love for us. Sexual intercourse can only reflect its true meaning when it is within marriage, where the couple has sincerely promised themselves to each other forever before God and the community. That is why the Church teaches that sexual intercourse outside of marriage is not part of God's design for human love.

A Full and Forever Love

Now, for many of us, this is a difficult teaching to accept, especially if we are heading for marriage and "feel" committed. But remember, our purpose here is to look beyond personal opinion and at God's intended design for our sexual expressions. Think for a moment, do you know a couple who was sexually active and ended up not getting married either by choice or because things did not "work out"? Although their love may have felt at some point like it was committed, unconditional and life-giving, it wasn't. In their actions of intercourse they may have intended a "full and forever" meaning, but the unconditional and undying commitment was not truly part of that relationship. In other words, the action (intercourse) took place before the relationship had grown to the point of a forever, unconditional commitment. (A question concerning marriages that end in divorce could be posed at this point, as the divorced couple was apparently unable to sustain such a commitment. The answer to this question is beyond the scope of our present discussion of pre-marital sex, but can be pursued in the publications listed in the resource section, Appendix B.)

We should say at this point that we pass no judgment on the actions of any person. While it is clear that sex is often too casual, we believe that many people who choose to have sex before marriage do not plan to end their relationship short of a lifetime commitment. We believe, however, that the true meaning of human sexuality has been lost, or at least is not fully understood in our society. Intimate sexual activity is mistakenly understood as something we "need" or must have lest we become inhibited, rigid, or "behind the times." Sexual intercourse is often portrayed as the result of uncontrollable passion rather than as a union which is the product of faithful and committed love.

All one has to do is scan the romance section of a bookstore, watch a few soap operas, tune into prime time TV or catch some music videos for a clear picture of what society believes to be the norm for sexual behavior and values. But it is well worth the effort to look beyond what the media portrays. In light of the above discussion, we invite you to consider the value of choosing to save sexual intimacy for marriage. When the Church's teaching is evaluated, along with a consideration of the frequent physical and psychological side-effects of pre-marital sexual activity (see Appendix A), we believe there is much wisdom in waiting until after the wedding.

Summary

The Church teaches that sexual intimacy is to be reserved for marriage. Only after the wedding—after we have developed, proclaimed and witnessed to the fully committed and unconditional nature of our love for one another—can such intimacy fulfill its God-given meaning. Sexual intercourse is meant to be a sign to the husband and wife that their love for each other is fully committed, faithful and life-giving, and that God's love remains the same for them.

There are many publications that you can read to develop a fuller picture of the Catholic Church's teachings about pre-marital sex and marriage, and references are provided in Appendix B. We hope that you will read at least some of these as part of your journey toward acquiring a truly informed conscience.

Cohabitation

Question: Over the last 30 years, what do rock and roll groups, personal computers, video stores, gourmet ice cream stores and cohabiting couples have in common?

Answer: Their numbers have increased dramatically.

In fact, between 1965 and 1985, the U.S. saw a 400% increase in the number of unmarried couples who lived together, with recent estimates that at least 17% of married couples lived together before they were married.[3] The U.S. Bureau of Census recorded a 37% increase in cohabiting couples between 1980 and 1986, with the number jumping from 1.6 million to 2.2 million.[4] Needless to say, that is a lot of people.

We would like to discuss cohabitation from two viewpoints: that of the Church and that of society. We invite you to investigate the issues involved from several sides and with an open mind. There are many reasons why some couples choose to live together. These include consolidating finances, the desire for more time together, or ease in planning the wedding if the couple intends to get married. Other reasons may include testing compatibility or trying to deepen a relationship.[5] In our discussion, by cohabitation, or "living together," we mean: A man and a woman who are not married to one another, living together in a relationship that is sexually active. Using this definition, we do not include roommates or couples who live together for practical reasons but who have chosen to abstain from sexual activity and stick to that decision.

The Church's Position

The Catholic Church teaches that couples should not cohabit before marriage. To begin exploring why, recall from our discussion of pre-marital sex the "meaning" of sexual intercourse: it is a symbol of a husband's and wife's total self-giving to each other. It is a sign of the couple's committed and faithful love for each other—a love which is unitive and open to new life—as well as a symbol of God's love for his people. In a similar way, marriage "means" something. It is more than just two people saying, "I love you," sharing a house, and having kids.

In the Catholic Church, marriage is one of the seven Sacraments. A Sacrament is a sign of God's love for us. It is an action or symbol which helps us to know how deep and permanent God's love is. In the Sacrament of

Marriage, we pledge ourselves fully to our spouse and enter into a union which is sacred and holy (it is not "given" to us by the priest or deacon), and in doing so, publicly vow to love each other in a way that is committed, unconditional and undying. As part of the ceremony, the Church community promises to walk in solidarity with us and support us in times of trial and stress. Just as there are signs for the other sacraments (water in Baptism, oil in Confirmation, the bread and wine in Holy Eucharist), it is our visible love for each other which serves as the sign of the Sacrament of Marriage. From the way in which we experience love on a human level we come to understand better how much God loves us on a divine level.

Married Love as a Sign of God's Love

To further understand this, think of the phrase, "God loves you." How would we possibly be able to understand what this means without having experienced love of some kind from another person? Unless we have felt cared for in a way that was committed, and without conditions, it is very difficult to fully grasp that God could love us in the same way.

Other people also see the love between us as husband and wife. Our relatives, friends, children and acquaintances, even strangers in a restaurant see our gentleness, mutual respect and the care we show for each other. The Church teaches that these signs serve as a mirror of God's love reflected to all people, and of Christ's love for the Church—permanent and life-giving.

The relationship between couples who cohabit does not reflect the kind of love that God intends marriage to possess. Couples who live together in this manner have not formally and publicly—before God and the Church community—promised their love to each other in a way that is committed, unconditional and open to new life. Their love reflects neither God's love for us nor Christ's love for his Church. While the couple may be living as if they are married, they are not, and so their relationship can't fulfill the meaning God has given to marriage—that of being a model of God's complete and permanent love for his people—and therefore the Church cannot permit cohabitation as an appropriate Christian lifestyle.

Research with Cohabiting Couples

As with issues of pre-marital sex, our experience is that many people do not find much "practical" wisdom in the Church's teaching regarding cohabitation. Aside from the more spiritual aspects which we have already discussed, we challenge you to rethink the "practical aspects" of cohabitation in light of recent research conducted on unmarried couples living together. These studies show that couples who live together, whether engaged or not, tend to be less committed in their relationships.[6] It appears that couples who cohabit have a lower rate of eventual marriage than couples who do not cohabit,[7] and their lower level of commitment is reflected in ways

such as being less likely to pool income, own joint property, and share in leisure activities. Of greatest concern, perhaps, is that they are less likely to think that being faithful to one partner is important.[8]

The impact of this less committed attitude can be seen in the divorce rates of couples who lived together before they were married. In one study of nearly 3000 marriages, couples who cohabited and then married had an 80% higher divorce rate than couples who lived apart before marriage.[9] In fact, couples who lived together for longer periods of time (three years or more), had a higher divorce rate than those who lived together for shorter periods of time. Other studies have supported the same correlation between cohabitation and relationship permanence,[10] which would suggest that living together before marriage does not necessarily lead to a more lasting, satisfying relationship. Instead, it appears that the degree of commitment expressed by couples who live together depends, for many, on the quality of the immediate relationship, not on the desire to pledge oneself to another for life.[11]

Communication and Coping

Statistics show that the length of time that relationships last between non-married men and women who live together is usually less than two years, with the median length being 1.3 years, and two out of five relationships ending within one year.[12] The reasons for such high rates of relationship instability are not clear, but our experience in working with engaged couples and couples seeking marriage counseling seem to reveal problems in two areas: poor communication, and a lack of skill or willingness to make adjustments and work through periods of relationship stress and disillusionment. The personality characteristics of the people involved obviously play a significant role here, but early sexual involvement also seems to hurt the development of skills necessary for communication and commitment.[13]

Sexual intercourse can sometimes serve as a mechanism to avoid dealing with uncomfortable relationship issues. It can inhibit the development of the ability to talk about difficult issues or the learning of ways to express love which are not sexual. We often have seen couples who believe that "if sex is OK, we're OK," even when they were truly struggling. Also, there appears to be a correlation between pre-marital sex and post-marital affairs, again, likely due to the attitudes that do not place priority on committed, faithful love. Sexual activity heightens the physical intensity of the relationship, making it difficult to be objective about the benefits and risks of choosing someone to be a lifelong partner. Simply sharing the same house, then, is not the sole focus of concern for cohabitation; the sexual involvement as well appears to backfire on the relationship stability.

Summary

God's plan, then, is for marriage and sexual intimacy to help the couple reach true human fulfillment. Through the witness of their love for one another, the couple helps all people come to know and understand God's love for them.

Cohabitation does not reflect this plan. Rather, it reflects the choices made by the couple to avoid an exclusive and permanent commitment to one another, and to avoid an exclusive and permanent commitment to God. They do not live as models of God's love for his people. Whereas pre-marital sexual activity can cloud the message of God's love for the individual man and woman, cohabitation also clouds the message of God's love for all his people.

Pope John Paul II has called living together outside of marriage an "experiment with human beings" as the couple tries out each other's suitability according to their own desires. This testing does not encourage deep levels of trust. The Pope reminds us that our human dignity demands that people should be "always and solely the term of a self-giving love without limitations of time or any other circumstances."[14] Cohabitation, in the Church's view, does not engender a love which is self-giving and without limitations.

We hope that you will pursue further understanding of the Church's teaching in this area by praying, talking to knowledgeable people, and reading. We hope, also, that should you be currently living together, considering doing so, or, if you have lived with someone in the past, that you will give these issues some thought and discussion. While the reasons and motivations surrounding a couple's choice to live together need to be respectfully processed and understood case by case, we hope that you will have the courage to look at your specific situation with the Church's teachings in mind. This may be difficult, but we believe that the challenge is worthwhile in many ways.

Contraception

An Overview

The Church's teaching on contraception is similar to parallel parking. Now, don't laugh. Most people like to drive, or at least they don't mind it, but most people do not like parallel parking. It's hard to do—especially in tight spaces with people watching. Can we drive on the highway? Easy. Drive in the rain? Easy. Drive in rush hour traffic while drinking a cup of coffee and eating a bagel? Easy. Parallel park? Not so easy.

Now take some of the teachings of the Catholic Church, like "Love thy neighbor." Can we agree with that? Easy. "Help the poor." Easy. "Go to church on Sunday." Uh, pretty easy. "Don't use contraceptive means to prevent pregnancy." Not so easy. Hence, the similarity between contraception and parallel parking.

The Catholic Church teaches that contraceptive choices are immoral. By "contraceptive choices" is meant any direct action which, either in anticipation of sexual intercourse, or once it has occurred, tries to render pro-creation impossible.[15] Our experience has been, however, that the subject of contraception is one of the most diffi-cult issues people have with Church teaching. It is more controversial than the subject of cohabitation (only 5% of men and women believe that cohabitation is a preferred lifestyle),[16] and tougher than the struggle with teachings on pre-marital sex (e.g., 50% of men and women agree that sex should be reserved for marriage).[17] Many Catho-lics either struggle with the teaching or reject it outright.

During our engagement, the contraception ques-tion created a good deal of tension and frustration as we simply were not sure what to do about it. In retrospect, our frustration was a result of two factors: 1. Not fully understanding why the Church forbids the use of con-traceptive methods, and 2. Not being aware of any rea-sonable/effective alternative family planning method that the Church had to offer. We found ourselves asking two questions: "Why not use contraceptive methods?" and "What does the Church have to offer us as an alterna-tive?"

In general, we've found these questions answered in this way:

1. The Church teaches that sexual intercourse has a twofold meaning: it is both unitive and "procreative" (open to new life). Contraception prevents intercourse from being procreative. This has negative physical, psy-chological, social and spiritual results.

2. The Church offers us the method of Natural Family Planning as an effective and morally acceptable means to be responsible parents.

In the sections that follow, we will try to share our understanding of the rationale behind these answers. We will begin with a bit of history.

A Historical Context

The teaching that contraception and abortion are not to be used as a means of regulating birth has been part of Christian doctrine since the early Church. (Actually, we can find a reference to contraception in the Old Testament, see Genesis 38:9-10.)[18] During the 16th century, Pope Sixtus V wrote of the moral difficulties inherent in the use of contraceptives.[19] Until 1930, the consensus of all Christian religions was that contraceptive use was not morally permissible. That year, however, with a document issued from the Lambeth Conference of 1930, the Anglican Church began to permit contraception. That same year, Pope Pius XI wrote the encyclical, *Casti Connubii*, to re-affirm the Catholic position that contraceptive means of birth control were against God's design for the order of creation. This has been restated in more recent years by Pope Paul VI in the encyclical letter *Humanae Vitae* (1968), and frequently by Pope John Paul II (e.g., *Familiaris Consortio*, 1981). Officially, then, the position of the Catholic Church on contraception has not changed over the years, although the debate continues to be a hot one. For many couples the question remains: "Why not?" The first part of the answer is that the Church believes that sexual intercourse must be procreative. Let's consider what that means.

The Meaning of "Procreative"

To understand where the Church is coming from on contraception, the term "procreative" plays a central role. As we said before, sexual intercourse has a "unitive" meaning—it unites us in love and deepens the commitment we have for each other. God also intends intercourse to have what is referred to as "procreative" meaning. Unfortunately, "procreative" is probably one of the most misunderstood words in Catholicism. Its use has led to the widely held belief that the Church wants us all to have families of ten children or more. It is this misconception which often leads to the whole of Catholic sexual teachings being thrown out. We see no sense in an institution that (we mistakenly believe) wants us to have large numbers of children regardless of our circumstances, and therefore we reject all Church teachings on sexual issues as being "out of touch."

Procreative actually means "open to life." When the Church teaches that each act of sexual intercourse must be procreative, it means that each act of sexual intercourse must be "open to life." The Church does not say that we should have as many children as we physically can, rather, she asks us to exercise "responsible parenthood."[20] This means that in decisions about family size, we take into account our financial, emotional, material, psychological, spiritual and social resources, and look at our ability to raise our children in light of this assessment. The decision is to be made, however, not on issues of convenience, but from the perspective of working with God and a desire to unselfishly love our children as gifts which he has entrusted to our guardianship.

In light of this, to be procreative, or open to life, means that we not do anything to consciously prevent the possibility of a child being conceived nor destroy life at any time after conception. (Choosing to refrain from intercourse during the fertile phase of a woman's cycle is discussed in the next chapter.) "Contraception" (against conception) is any choice which impedes or alters the natural possibility of conception. The following are some of the more common means of either preventing conception (i.e., fertilization), or preventing the birth of any already conceived child:

—Altering a woman's natural hormonal cycle to prevent pregnancy, via the pill, chemical implants, etc.

—Altering a man's sperm production or transportation via vasectomy, chemical means, etc.

—Preventing the growth to term of a conceived child via abortion, RU486, the pill, IUD, etc.

—The withdrawal of the penis and ejaculation outside the vagina (*coitus interruptus*).[21]

In other words, contraception is anything we choose to do which purposefully changes God's plan for the way human life is to be transmitted or reproduced. In the following sections of this chapter we will discuss some of the reasons why using contraceptives contradict both the unitive and the procreative meaning of sexual intercourse.

Physical Consequences

Although an unpopular topic, we face the reality that our attempts to change God's design for sexual intercourse have resulted in many physical health concerns. We believe it is essential to be aware of the physical consequences of contraceptives before any choice regarding their use is made. This knowledge is especially important for women, who primarily experience these dangers. The following list is not exhaustive, but consider these known side effects from some of the more commonly used contraceptives:

Loestrin, Low Estrogen Pill: Stroke due to brain hem-

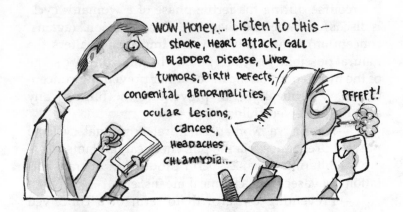

orrhage: 2x greater risk than nonusers; stroke due to blood clot: 4–9.5x greater risk; heart attack: 2x greater risk for non-smokers, 10–12x greater risk for smokers. Also an increased risk of thrombosis; gall bladder disease; tumors of the liver; birth defects and congenital abnormalities, including heart and lung defects if used while pregnant (e.g., the damage may occur even before you know you are pregnant); ocular lesions; cancer; increased blood pressure; headaches; bleeding irregularities; ectopic pregnancy; reduced beta-carotene (inhibits tumor growth); chlamydia and gonnococcal infection. After discontinuing the pill, there is the increased risk of cerebrovascular disease (e.g., stroke) which remains for six years; the increased risk of a heart attack remains for up to nine years.[22, 23, 24]

Spermicides, diaphragm show an increased risk of: preeclampsia (pregnancy disorder).[25]

Condoms show an increased risk of: preeclampsia; contact urticaria (allergic reaction); AIDS (due to condom failure to completely inhibit the virus).[26, 27, 28]

Vasectomy may result in the increased risk of prostate cancer.[29]

Again, this list is not complete, but it does provide some insight as to the negative physical impact that contraceptives can have. And, again we point out that it is most often women who suffer the negative physical side effects.

While the Church does not see side effects such as these as "punishment from God" for muscling in on his turf (human reproduction, that is), these health concerns do tell us that contraceptives don't mix well with the natural biological processes of our bodies. Our choice to use them challenges God's desire for us to respect the natural order of creation; they do not allow us to work with God as co-creators of human life. They alter God's physical design for intercourse and/or fertility, and the Church cannot support their use. Instead, the choice of many couples to space, and at times even to limit, the conception of children through the practice of Natural Family Planning (discussed in the next chapter) *is* permissible. It both respects and works in conjunction with the natural processes of our bodies.

Psychological and Social Consequences

To appreciate the negative impact contraception has in psychological and social areas, it helps to understand that the unitive and procreative meanings of sex are permanently linked. Since one flows from the other, the Church teaches that if we eliminate the procreative aspect of intercourse through contraception, we diminish/lower the ability of sex to unite us at the deepest levels of love that God intends us to experience. The reason for this is that contraception prevents truly unconditional love. Here's how:

Think of someone you love or care deeply about. Perhaps that person is your spouse-to-be, your boyfriend or girlfriend, etc. Now, if there is something about their body you wish were different, do you insist they change it before you will love them?

—If his/her ears are too big, do you make him/her have them reduced?

—If he or she is too heavy, do you insist he/she lose weight before you will love him/her?

—If his or her nose is too long, do you hold back your love until he/she gets a nose job?

Hopefully, you answered "No." If you answer "Yes," you are saying that your love for this person is conditional, making it dependent on some physical trait. Unconditional love, on the other hand, does not let being overweight, having big ears or a big nose stop you from loving a person.

Contraceptive methods of birth control, however, create an atmosphere of conditional love because the giving of our love in intercourse depends on us changing something about ourselves. (Remember, one of the intrinsic purposes of sexual intimacy is that it be a sign of our unconditional love for each other.) Without the couple's reflecting on it perhaps, sexual intercourse using contraceptives is conditional; we express our love sexually to our partner only if something is different about them, namely, that their life-giving ability is altered. It does not signify unconditional love.

Intercourse is supposed to say, "I give you all of me," and/or "I receive all of you without conditions." Intercourse using contraceptives says, "Well, I choose not to give you all of me," and/or "I don't want to receive all of you." If we use a contraceptive we hold back part of ourselves and sexual intimacy becomes a sign of conditional love, the condition being, "I will show you my love only if we can change you or intercourse in some way so we don't have a child." The union is not "complete"—there is some physical, God-given part of our body that we do not share with the other. Admittedly, this is heady stuff, but let's try to look at it from a practical perspective.

Would it make sense to say any of these to the person we love?

"I love you, but I'll only show my love for you if you use a condom and keep your sperm to yourself."

"I love you, but I won't show my love for you unless you use this pill and turn off your estrogen for a few weeks."

"I love you, but I won't show my love for you until you get your tubes tied / have your vas deferens snipped."

Whether such conditions make sense or not is what *you* are challenged to decide, but we don't see such bargains as reflective of unconditional love.

Follow the logic of this "take all of me" thinking:

Scenario A

My body is part of "me." The ability to conceive a child results from our bodily union, so the ability I have to contribute to conception can be said to be part of me.

If I somehow suppress/withhold/remove my body's ability to contribute to the conception of a child before or during intercourse, I have suppressed/withheld/removed part of me from that experience.

God asks that sexual intercourse be an expression of total and unconditional love.

Since contraceptives suppress/withhold/remove my ability to contribute to the conception of a child, which is part of my body, which is part of me, I am not giving *all of me* to my spouse if I use them.

Scenario B

My spouse's body is part of my spouse.

My spouse's ability to contribute to the conception

of a child is part of my spouse's body, so it, too, can be said to be part of my spouse.

If my spouse somehow suppresses/withholds/removes his or her ability to contribute to the conception of a child before or during intercourse, he or she has suppressed/withheld/removed part of himself or herself from that experience.

God asks that when we have sexual intercourse, I unconditionally receive *all of my spouse.*

Since contraceptives suppress/withhold/remove my spouse's ability to conceive a child, which is part of my spouse's body, which is part of my spouse, I am not receiving *all of my spouse* if I use them.

According to Church teaching, therefore, intercourse that utilizes contraception is not an act of unconditional, self-giving love and is contrary to God's intent. God, through Jesus, held none of himself back from us. Since our love is meant to be a reflection of God's love, God does not want us to withhold any part of ourselves from each other. (There are certainly instances where contraceptives are prescribed for medical reasons which are not contraceptive in nature. Such cases require a discussion beyond our present scope. However, the issues involved can be pursued in the resources listed in Appendix B.)

The Contraceptive Attitude

The withholding of part of ourselves as described above can lead to what is referred to as a "contraceptive attitude." Such an attitude says: "Just as part of me can be withheld in sex, other parts of me can be withheld in other areas of our relationship." In other words, if I believe that it is OK to hold back part of me in the sexual realm, then it is OK to hold back other parts of me, such as: my thoughts, my fears, my anger, my guilt, my listening, my support, my willingness to challenge you.

A contraceptive attitude is one in which love in other areas of the relationship also becomes conditional, such as:

I'll forgive him *if* he says he's sorry.

I'm not going to listen to her *unless* she listens to me.

I won't ask about his day *until* he asks about mine.

If she won't be more friendly toward my family, I won't be friendly toward hers.

Statements and attitudes similar to these are familiar to all of us, and, again, reflect a withholding on our part. Whether consciously or unconsciously, these attitudes "contracept" the communication in our relationships; we have stopped being open to life—the life of our relationship as well as the possible transmission of new life. Decision-making, communication, household responsibilities, money, family, religion, social activities... all are arenas in which being "closed to life," or suppressing (or withholding or removing) our honest thoughts, feelings and actions can be hurtful to our relationships. Such an attitude is often rooted in being closed to life in our sexual relationship, that is, in the use of contraceptives.

Now, we are not saying that the action of inserting a diaphragm, or taking a pill, or having a vasectomy, magically creates an attitude which can hurt our relationships. It is not the product or operation that is our focus here, rather it is the thinking behind the use of the product or of having the operation that can lead to difficulties. It is an attitude which believes that it is OK for us to keep part of ourselves out of the relationship with the person we love.

The psychological impact experienced by persons in relationships which are closed due to such attitudes is great and can include decreased self-esteem, lack of trust, anger, hurt, depression and a sense of rejection. Society is hurt through the negative impacts of these psychological effects on children and family life. In addition, as the availability and use of contraceptives has increased since the 1960's, so have the rates of divorce, which causes us to wonder about the possibility of a correlation between the two. When we consider that the highest rates of divorce occur among couples who have *chosen* not to have children,[30] the impact of contraception and the contraceptive attitude becomes something for all of us to think about.

While there are many factors contributing to the increasing numbers of abortions (e.g., legalization, growth of the abortion business, etc.), research is also showing a connection between the use of contraceptives and abortion. As contraceptives have been made increasingly available, U.S. government statistics show that the abortion rate has actually increased for teenage women from 19.22 per 1000 women in 1972 to 46.20 per 1000 in 1985.[31,32] Data shows that approximately one half of all women who have had abortions were using some form of contraceptive at the time of conception.[33] The concern here is twofold. First, when contraceptives fail, abortion is used as the back-up contraceptive method. Second, the nature of some contraceptives is to act as abortifacients causing the abortion of an unborn child. The latter include the IUD, RU486 and the pill.[34]

To sum up, the Catholic Church teaches that each act of sexual intercourse should be a sign of our unconditional love for each other and reflect God's unconditional love for us. Allowing intercourse to be procreative or open to life leads us to feel a deeper love for one another and to participate more fully in God's creation of new life. The Church objects to the use of contraceptives because they prevent intercourse from being open to life and place sex in an arena of conditional love. The Church is also concerned about the potential for a contraceptive attitude to develop in our relationships. Such an attitude hurts us individually in psychological ways and also affects society in general by undermining the strength of marriage and family life.

Spiritual Consequences

What is the most important reason why the Church teaches that sexual intercourse should remain open to life? The answer is that by doing so we respect God's authority over life and increase our trust in him. Consider for a moment relationships like parent and child, coach and player, teacher and student. We would generally agree that a healthy respect for the authority of the person in charge, as well as a sense of trust in him or her, usually leads to positive results. In the area of sexuality, we see God as our "coach" and try to respect his "plans," trusting that they will bring us good results. The Church teaches that respect and trust in God's design are necessary to help us know and experience a full union with him. The Church is concerned that the use of

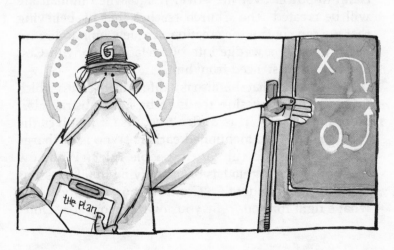

contraceptives and the "contraceptive mentality" can affect us spiritually. In other words, using them can hurt our relationship with God.

Pause here and reflect for a moment on the phrase "relationship with God." For many of us this is a difficult concept. Often in our growing up we grouped "the Church, religion, and faith" all together, and not much time was spent encouraging us to nurture a relationship with God. We learned about the Church's structure, rules and history, but not always about how to love the Lord. Yet having this relationship, and understanding just what that relationship is, is central to gaining insight into contraception's spiritual consequences. Our goal here is to move beyond a simple "not following the rules" perspective to a deeper "hurting my relationship with God" level of awareness.

Consider this: If we respect and trust God when it comes to the question of having children, then what we are saying is that we understand how he made our bodies to work. We trust that when and if a child is conceived, he has plans for that life and is entrusting us with it. Contraception, however, is our way of laying claim to power over life—over if and when human life will be created. The Church teaches that by believing that we can control the creation of a new human life we begin to drive a wedge into our relationship with God and become distanced from him.

We realize that this also is a difficult area with which to deal. The discussion tends to be a bit abstract, but more importantly, it is difficult because it involves the core questions we mentioned earlier: "Who is in charge here?" "Does God rule or do people rule?" We know that our own struggle has been in trying to take lessons like "Be independent," "Control your destiny," "Do what's right for you," "Be your own person," or "Don't be a conformist," and merge these with "Do what the Church says," or "Trust the Lord's plan for you." We've often said things like, "Oh, what does the Church know?" or, "Where does it say that in the Bible?" And we know we're not alone. Because the spiritual issues involved in the Church's teaching on contraception are a bit tough to read through, we will try to address them as concretely as we can.

Adam and Eve and the Struggle for Power. To begin exploring God's answer to the question, "Who has authority over human life?" let's look at Genesis and the story of Adam and Eve. Most of us are familiar with the story: Part I—God creates Adam and Eve, they live in Paradise. Part II—They eat the forbidden fruit. Part III—God finds out and sends them out of the Garden. Pretty basic.

Remember the expression, "Can't see the forest for the trees?" In our case, we can't deal completely with the spiritual consequences of the contraception message without considering the trees in the Garden! If you re-read the creation stories as told from Genesis 1–3:24, you will

note that Adam and Eve had every good thing in the Garden. Their "vocation" if you will was twofold: They were created in the image of God, and they were the caretakers of the rest of creation. The only directive which the Creator imposed was that they should not eat of the Tree of Knowledge of Good and Evil. As best as we can tell, they were peaceful and had no problems or conflicts. They were in harmonious union with God and with each other.

Eventually, however, Adam and Eve ate from the Tree of Knowledge. Then they became aware of the difference between good and evil, immediately experiencing difficult human emotions like guilt, embarrassment and anxiety. (So, even before God sent them out of the Garden, they had "fallen" from their state of peace and harmony.)

What exactly was the "wrong" done? Aside from the literal act of disobedience, Adam and Eve had taken for themselves a power belonging properly to the Creator—the power to name good and evil. God's "comment" as we continue the story is that Adam and Eve must leave the Garden before they eat from "the Tree of Life." You see, Adam and Eve (and all of us) were called to image (or reflect) God to one another and to all of creation. But we ourselves are *not* God; in that original act of disobedience by Adam and Eve, our image/reflection of God was shattered. Instead of living out the vocation for which we were created, we seek vainly to have the power of God. We desire to name for ourselves what is good and what is evil.[35]

Contraception as a Spiritual Power Struggle. From this perspective, contraception is our attempt to say to God, "Hey, people rule. What you or the Church say is just an opinion, so we can act according to our opinion and change both the ways we have intercourse and our bodies' abilities to conceive children. We will decide what is good and what is evil. We will decide when life will be created, not you."

The Church, in contrast, asks that we admit instead, "God rules. He has ultimate power and authority over the creation of human life and, out of respect for that authority, we choose to keep intercourse open to life." The Church sees this route as helping us to grow closer to God as it allows us to work *with* him in the creation of life. The other route moves us away from God as we try to take upon ourselves the power to create or to destroy a person. On a much smaller scale, we can compare it to what happens when a young child tries to take control from his parents; when a player tries to take control from the coach; when the student tries to take control from the teacher. The results can be hurtful, even disastrous.

What we often don't remember among all of the "don'ts" is that God meant sexual intimacy to be wonderful. It is a total, unconditional self-giving of ourselves to one another which reflects God's total self-giving to us. It is a way of learning how love can be complete. Sexual intimacy is the loving expression of a union which is physical, psychological, social and spiritual. When the life of a child results from the action of sexual intercourse, a new human person starts on his or her spiritual journey toward union with God. Hence, this sharing of love is also a very spiritual process. The Church cannot approve of our using contraceptive methods as these inherently reflect an "equal to God" attitude.

A Breather... Remember how Jack Nicholson looked in *One Flew Over the Cuckoo's Nest* after he had the frontal lobotomy? He was a zombie. He was disconnected from the meaning of life. In the Church's view, contraception performs a lobotomy on human sexuality by disconnecting the spiritual essence from the physical, psychological and social components. Human sexuality, says Pope John Paul II in *Familiaris Consortio*, "is an enrichment of the whole person—body, mind and soul, and it manifests its inmost meaning in leading the person to the gift of self in love."[36] Contraception runs counter to this design.

Summary

We can sum up the Church's teaching on contraception in this way: Sexual intercourse is the most intimate and powerful way in which we can show one another how committed, unconditional and life-giving our love for one another is. It is also a way of experiencing God's committed, unconditional and life-giving love for each of us, and so it must allow for the possibility of a child to be conceived as a fruit of that love. With contraceptives, intercourse is not open to life. Its not being open to life can lead to significant negative effects on the physical, psychological, social and spiritual levels.

Heavy stuff, we know, but important stuff. We've made a sincere attempt not to pass moral judgment on

anyone who uses or plans to use contraception. As we said at the outset, it is the responsibility of each of us to learn what God desires in issues of sexual morality and make choices based on that information. This book is about such information; it is not about judgment. Jesus' message was love, not tar and feathering.

With this in mind, we hope you will ask yourself some important questions as you consider your own relationship decisions. Some examples might be: Are we working in tandem with God's plan for us? Do our decisions take into account the fullest aspect of giving ourselves totally to one another? Do our decisions have the dimension of unconditional love?

Maybe the clearest question at this point of our discussion is, "OK, great. So what are we supposed to do if we cannot responsibly provide for a large number of children?" Answer: Natural Family Planning.

Natural Family Planning

Our Experience

Five months prior to our wedding, having researched and ruled out all of the contraceptives on the market, we felt very much like Laurel and Hardy—we looked at each other and asked, "What do we do now, Ollie?" It was not a comfortable feeling.

now WHat, OLLie?

At that point, a couple whom we knew asked us if we would be interested in hearing about Natural Family Planning (hereafter referred to as NFP). They had been using NFP since she had stopped using the pill (due to health-related problems). Initially, we were skeptical of a birth regulating method which did not rely on a prescription or manufacturing plant, but we soon found out that NFP was more than simply a reliable method of postponing pregnancy—it is a method of family planning and a way of life which has enriched our relationship. Perhaps more importantly for our present discussion, NFP is also the family planning method promoted by the Catholic Church; it is based on living within God's designs for marriage and human sexuality.

The Method

Briefly, NFP is a technique used to identify the days in a woman's menstrual cycle during which she is fertile (could conceive a new life). On these days we consciously make the choice to have intercourse if conception is desired, or to abstain from intercourse if conception is not desired at that time.

In the course of a woman's cycle, her body goes through physical changes that indicate whether she is fertile or infertile (cannot conceive a new life). Three main signs are tracked: basal body temperature (body temperature at the time you wake up), cervical mucus, and actual changes in the position and texture of the cervix. These signs, which are controlled by changes in the female hormones, are observed and recorded by the couple. After learning how to pinpoint the fertile times, the wife and husband *together* decide whether or not to have intercourse (depending on whether or not they want to possibly conceive a child at that time). In this way, the choice of when to have sexual intercourse and for spacing pregnancies does not fall to one spouse alone, the decisions are constantly, mutually shared.

There are different methods of NFP. One method focuses primarily on temperature changes, another looks primarily for changes in cervical mucus (called the Ovulation or Billings Method). We use and are most familiar with the "Sympto-thermal" method, which is based on the three signs mentioned above. (References for the different methods are provided in Appendix B.)

We *Don't* Have "RHYTHM"

NFP is *not* the "Rhythm Method" familiar to our parents, grandparents and the secular press. "Rhythm" basically involved guessing at fertile times and planning

intercourse on either side of them. The guess was based on the assumption that all women have regular menstrual cycles, which, unfortunately, made the method only as good as the guess. NFP, instead, is scientific, well researched, and systematically taught; it is not a method of hit and miss.

We *Do* Plan with God

A common question about NFP is: "But isn't it still contraception? You're trying not to get pregnant, aren't you? Doesn't the Church say *no* birth control?"

Remember, the Church has never said that we must have as many kids as possible. The Church is well aware that to be responsible parents we need—for many reasons—to space the birth of children. Responsible parenthood involves choices about how many children to have and when to have them. The issue, then, isn't whether or not planning your family is permissible, it is an issue of how to plan in a way which is respectful of both the unitive and the procreative dimensions of sexual intercourse; of how to live marriage and family life in accordance with our Christian faith and the natural law.

Contraception purposefully tries to *block* the possibility of a new life, or to destroy that life at its first moments of existence. With NFP, on the other hand, we identify the times when *God* has made us fertile via the woman's menstrual cycle, and then choose accordingly to have or not to have sexual intercourse. NFP does not require a choice against the procreative (open to life) or the unitive (fully self-giving) dimension of sexual intercourse. NFP enables us to use our human powers of self-awareness and self-control to freely choose our actions.

An Example. We can think of the difference between planning with God and without God in this way:

You like to hike in the woods near the seashore. The "developer" of the woods says you can hike there, and the design of the woods includes the presence of a beautiful salt marsh full of fish and wildlife which you are invited to enjoy. During certain high tides, the sea water flows several feet over the hiking trail near the marsh. At those times you must wade through some very deep water. However, that is the best time to survey the fish and wildlife.

Now, even though you really love to see the wildlife, you know you will not always be prepared to do any wading. However, you've learned through a method of careful observation that the high tide only flows over the hiking trail one week out of each month and you have been able to accurately chart which week this is. Some months there may be slight variations in which the tide's "flooding week" starts and ends, but your observation system can detect those variations.

Here are your options:

1. At those times when you are not prepared to go wading, do something different the week that the high tide is present, and hike during the three weeks out of each month that the water is not flooding over the trail.

2. Stop the tide from entering the marsh all month long by building a dam upstream and hiking whenever you want. (You may not ever enjoy the fish and other wildlife, in fact they may die, but at least you can hike.)

In option one, you respect the natural rhythm of the tide and the developer's design of the woods, enjoying the wildlife at high tide only when you are prepared to do so.

In option two, you change the developer's design

by removing what you don't want (i.e., having to wade through the water).

Both succeed in allowing you to hike and not wade, but clearly the methods and the intentions are quite different. Hopefully, we would choose the first option—working within the designs of the developer by respecting the natural properties of the established design. The second option—changing the design according to how we want it—does not respect the natural design and plan of the developer. This is basically the logic behind the Church's teaching on responsible parenting: Marriage and sexual intercourse are designed to be unitive and procreative. If you wish to avoid pregnancy, plan sexual intercourse for the times when the natural rhythms of human fertility will not result in pregnancy.

In the above example:
Sexual intercourse is "hiking."
God is the developer.
Human sexuality is the woods.
Fertility/pregnancy is wading in the marsh at high tide.
NFP is the method of careful observation.
Infertile periods of a woman's menstrual cycle are the three weeks of lower tides.
The fertile period of a woman's menstrual cycle is the one week of highest tides.
Other ways of showing love is the "doing something else."
Contraception is building the dam.

Does NFP Work?

The obvious question becomes, "Does NFP work?" Is it effective? The answer is "Yes." It is very effective. Research studies have shown the effectiveness of the

NFP method to be 97-99%, or a "failure rate" of 1-3%.[37, 38] Consider this along side "effectiveness rates" for contraceptives.

Effectiveness Rates of Birth Control Methods
(in percents)[39, 40, 41, 42, 43]

> Pill 92-98%
> Sterilization-Male 98-99%
> Sterilization-Female 96-99%
> IUD 94-95%
> Condom 85-90%
> Spermicides 75-92%
> Sponge 78-90%
> Cervical Cap 87-92%
> NFP 97-99%

These again are *method* effectiveness rates. The actual *user* effectiveness rates (how well people practice the method) are actually lower, and they are more difficult to statistically determine. User effectiveness rates are particularly lower for methods which relate directly to sexual activity, such as condoms, diaphragms, spermicides, sponge, etc.[44] As with any method, NFP itself must be learned and practiced consistently in order to have maximum effectiveness.

It is important to note that in many secular publications NFP is generally referred to as "periodic abstinence." This label is used to describe any method based on the monitoring of bodily signs and/or the old "rhythm" method. Because of the scientific nature of NFP, its methods of observation, training and practice, as well as its inherent spiritual values, it is a misnomer to merely classify it as a method of contraception called "periodic abstinence."[45]

Side Effects of NFP

NFP does not have negative physical side effects associated with it as do the forms of contraception discussed in the last chapter. It is our opinion, moreover, that just by keeping the "artificial" stuff out and allowing our bodies to operate naturally is in itself a healthy physical "side effect."

On the psychological, social and spiritual levels, NFP also provides positive benefits rather than negative side effects. Results from studies conducted with NFP users, for example, show that NFP couples have higher levels of self-esteem and spiritual well-being than couples who use oral contraceptives.[46] Studies have also shown that NFP has a positive impact on the overall quality of couples' relationships, while the use of oral contraceptives may have a negative impact.[47] In regard to social effects, divorce rates of couples who use NFP have been found to be 10% or less.[48] Compare this with divorce rates in general, which are hovering around 48-52%.

Why should NFP have positive effects on a person's psychological, social and spiritual well-being? Because

self-awareness, self-acceptance and self-control are integral to the method. After using NFP for eleven years, we have experienced in ourselves an improved awareness of how our bodies work. We recognize a greater appreciation and acceptance of how we can work with God to bring new life into the world, and a greater ability to be self-disciplined. Put these together and the resulting sense of self-worth and mutual respect spills into everything we do. Research—as well as our experience with other NFP-using couples—points to the same conclusion. In fact, one man involved in the pioneering of the pill has begun to advocate the positive benefits of "fertility awareness."[49]

Lower divorce rates and more fulfilling relationships also result from using NFP as it helps prevent the "contraceptive attitude" discussed earlier. Keeping sexual intimacy open to life keeps intercourse complete in its ability to communicate that sense of unconditional love as we give and receive "all" of one another. This complete sense of acceptance also carries over into other areas of our relationship and helps us survive the inevitable times of stress and disillusionment in marriage.

NFP has also kept our relationship growing as it requires mutual responsibility and frequent, open communication about very intimate matters. This is good practice for us as it has helped to sharpen our skills for communication on other subjects. Like every other couple, we still have our rough times, but the communication required as part of NFP has often helped to bring us back on track. Through NFP we have also developed a greater appreciation for the gift and meaning of our sexuality that we would not have found with other methods.

NFP also adds to our relationship the positive dimension of re-experiencing some of the joy that we felt on our honeymoon in anticipation of sexual intimacy.

Periods of sexual abstinence help to increase our appreciation for our sexual love-making and prevent us from taking one another for granted. Since we are able to identify the times of fertility, the planning for intercourse and the intimacy we share during the times in which we hope to conceive take on an extra dimension of power and beauty. The presence of God in our sexual relationship and our privilege to serve as co-creators of life becomes clear on these occasions and adds to the awareness of the gift of life which the Creator shares with us.

There are many other spiritual benefits resulting from the practice of NFP that you can explore through the references listed (see Appendix B), but we would like to emphasize two in particular:

1. Since the ability to conceive is never willfully eliminated, sexual intercourse maintains its spiritual dimension and makes it difficult for us to take sex for granted. Relationships can be strained when the only interest in sexual intimacy is a selfishly physical one. NFP provides a framework to keep our sexual appreciation for one another alive. Sexual intimacy remains an

expression of mutual respect and of self-donation, never of using each other merely for physical pleasure. This serves to deepen our trust and commitment to one another.

2. NFP allows us to come to know God more deeply and grow in our relationship with him. God is Love—a love that is unconditional and life-giving for each of us. It is through our love for one another that we can feel the depth of God's love for us. The NFP method provides us with the means to grow in love for self and our spouse, and as this love grows, so will our love for God. It is with this goal in mind that the Catholic Church offers us its teachings on responsible parenthood and the regulation of birth.

Summary

What we have attempted to do in this chapter is provide an overview of NFP and how its practice has enriched us on many levels. Obviously, there is much more to the physical and spiritual dimensions of NFP than we have mentioned here, but our intention is to be a springboard, not an end-all. It is also important to note that, as with all family planning methods, there are challenges inherent in it. Choosing not to have sex during a fertile time, for example, can be difficult when we are feeling sexually aroused or when things like anniversaries fall during a fertile phase. But, again, the challenge is to grow in those choices by finding other ways of experiencing and communicating our love for each other. Also, NFP must be learned thoroughly and practiced consistently in order to be effective, and that requires self-discipline and commitment.

In our marriage, however, all of these challenges seem to be helping us become better people and better spouses. We don't see them as clouds which darken the sexual part of our lives, but we see them, instead, as sign posts along the journey of our marriage which guide us to new depths of love for each other and for God.

Intimate Bedfellows: Sex and Faith

Keeping the Doors Open

"Oh, yes, yes...right there, honey, oh, a little higher.... Perrrfect!" And with that, the kitchen clock was hung.

Isn't it funny how certain words lead us to form certain pictures in our minds? Odds are, as you read the first sentence, you weren't thinking of a clock or a kitchen. For many, the words "sex" and "Catholic Church" have often produced a mental picture of repression, guilt, duty and rigidity. It is our hope that the preceding pages have helped to paint a different backdrop on the "sex and Church" canvas—one of joy, fulfillment, love and unity. We are well aware of the struggles which many of us feel in trying to bring together God, Church, love and sex, and hope that you will continue in your search for the threads of truth that can weave them into one understanding.

Perhaps our greatest sadness in dealing with issues of sexual morality occurs when discomfort with the topic leads some of us to become disconnected from the Church, or worse yet, from God. There has been a long history of debate over sexual issues (especially contraception), and there will likely be more discussion in the years ahead. Our prayer is that you will see decisions in these areas as a process of continuing discernment and not close the doors should you feel that you and the Church are rowing in the opposite direction. Answers and understanding are possible, but require personal effort, reading and talking to informed priests, religious men and women, and married couples with whom you can relate openly and share your struggles.

Quite contrary to what we were initially led to believe, celibate persons can have a great deal to share in the understanding of our sexuality. Just as we pledge ourselves unconditionally to our spouses in a way that calls for fidelity between the two of us, celibate persons have pledged unconditional faithfulness to God. In doing so, their commitment mirrors and supports our marriage vows. Although they are not bringing forth children, their fidelity to God brings forth new spiritual life in themselves and in those whom they serve. This celibate fidelity is often a very intimate process. To see celibacy as equivalent to ignorance of sexual issues is not an accurate generalization and we encourage you to talk with committed celibates. Their insights in the area of human sexuality can be invaluable in your search for answers and understanding.

A Matter of Faith

Central to the whole process of understanding and decision-making will be your personal relationship with God. When we boil down the issues of truth, conscience, sexual morality, contraception, cohabitation, etc., into a common core, we find that it is a spiritual thread which holds them all together. Simply put, it is a matter of faith. This, frankly, is often hard for us "show me" type people who need facts, figures and research studies to "prove" what is true. Just like the actors in the old Wendy's hamburger commercial, we can get caught up in asking, "Where's the beef?" Translated, that becomes,

"Where's the proof that these Church teachings are reasonable and really reflect the truth?"

We often look for the kind of research "beef" that would show us the certain proof of why sex should be saved for marriage; the clear evidence of why couples should not live together before they get married; the solid data that "proves" why NFP is the best way to fulfill our responsibilities in the transmission of life. The odds are, however, that we won't find such "beef" in the near future.

Problems with Research. There is a good reason why we won't soon find the beef. Because of the nature of the issues involved, fool-proof laboratory studies which randomly assign couples to the experimental and control groups necessary to draw scientific conclusions just can't be conducted. We can't, for example, pick couples who come to their parish priest to get married and say, "Couple #1, you use the pill; Couple #2, you use NFP; Couple #3, you live together before the wedding; Couple #4, you start having sex tonight." We can do studies after the fact, but because there are many and varying

factors which lead couples to choose different lifestyles, it is hard to get scientifically clear answers.

Problems in the way research is designed is not the only road block for us fact-seekers. Research on topics like these is rarely free from the influence of the personal values held by the people doing the research. Research on human reproduction and other sexual issues is often sponsored by businesses and social agencies who have a lot of money riding on the publication of information which supports their own agenda. (Could we ever imagine a pharmaceutical company or Planned Parenthood advocating no sexual activity before marriage? Or promoting the use of NFP? Not likely.) In this booklet, we have been very clear about our own bias and personal values which favor Church teachings. We don't pretend to hide it. But we don't think that God hides his intentions for love and life either, so we guess we're in good company. Still, though, we'd love to see "all the facts."

The Search for Truth

Sometimes we wonder if Jesus was talking about us when he said: "O Father, Lord of heaven and earth, thank you for hiding the truth from those who think themselves so wise, and for revealing it to little children" (cf Mt 11:25).

Little children take things on faith, they don't ask for the latest statistical data. We wish that we could be more like that and not be so information-needy, yet, that is often how we are. What Jesus seems to be affirming in the above prayer is that the conditions for a close relationship with him are not so much in our heads as in our hearts. That is why the issue of informed conscience is so important. It is only in a fully informed conscience that we can "feel" the presence of Jesus guiding us in the decisions we make. In truth, he does not sit on our shoulder, he lives within us. Our challenge is to take the information we learn from the world around us and try to integrate it with our internal awareness of Jesus.

This is why we say that although the moral struggles of today are partly physical, psychological and social, they are primarily spiritual in nature. All of our "parts" connect at the essence of what it means to be human—to be able to know God and live our lives in a loving relationship with him.

Where will this faith-journey regarding our sexuality take us? We don't know; but we do know that faith in God, faith in Jesus' love, faith in the wisdom of the Holy Spirit, and faith in the teaching magisterium of the Church will bring us to the truth we seek.

The Mystery of the Mask

Our intent throughout this book has been to serve as a starting point in understanding why the Catholic Church teaches what it does about pre-marital sex, cohabitation and contraception. If we have been able to unmask a small portion of the mystery behind these teachings, then this has been worthwhile. If we have been able to help paint the Church's views on sex and sexuality in a frame that sees sexual intimacy within marriage as a beautiful, pleasurable, creative, enriching and unifying aspect of our lives, then we have been all the more successful.

Just as the Lone Ranger left behind a silver bullet as a reminder of what he stood for, the readings listed in Appendix B can provide further insights into what the Church stands for in the area of sexual morality. We hope that you will read them.

We have always thought it unfortunate that the people in the Lone Ranger's time never were able to know the real man behind the mask. Luckily for us,

Jesus never wore a mask. If we can be open to his Spirit and pursue a closer relationship with him, Jesus has promised that we will come to know him and to know his love for us. It is this intimate union with Jesus which the Church tries to promote through its teachings by fostering a deeper, more intimate union between husband and wife.

The greatest challenge of our journey through life is to keep it one of love, and it is the presence of Jesus that helps keep this journey on course. May he travel with you on yours.

Appendix A

Negative Consequences of Sex Before Marriage

1. Physical Consequences
   a. Sexually transmitted diseases (chlamydia, herpes, syphilis, AIDS)
   b. Cervical cancer
   c. Pregnancy
   d. Possible sterility, infection from contraceptive use and abortion
2. Psychological Consequences
   a. Guilt
   b. Anxiety/fear of pregnancy, AIDS, etc.
   c. Disappointment
   d. Anger at self and others
   e. Hurt due to being used/using others
   f. Lowered self-esteem
3. Social Consequences
   a. Marrying the wrong person
   b. Clinging to someone because you thought that having sexual intercourse together meant that you were in love
   c. Focusing too much on the physical part of a relationship which blocks emotional closeness and increases the risk of relationships breaking up

  d. Possible limits placed on the development of communication skills

Positive Consequences of Saving Sex for Marriage

1. Early sexual involvement risks lowering self-esteem, saving sexual involvement for marriage boosts self-esteem.

2. Self-esteem can be thought of as having three parts: self-awareness, self-control and self-respect. Holding off on sex boosts all three.

  a. It builds self-awareness as you focus more on relating verbally and emotionally.

  b. It builds self-control because it is hard to keep sexual urges in perspective, and when we choose to control them we build our image in the areas of self-control, self-discipline and the ability to rise above strong urges.

  c. It builds self-respect as a result of a and b.

Other Benefits of Saving Sex

1. It allows for freedom to follow life/career/educational plans.

2. It allows for the time and creates the need to develop skills for emotional intimacy and respect for the opposite sex.

  a. It can be compared to learning to drive: we don't just jump in a car the first time and "floor it." It takes time to build skills for safe driving.

  b. Refraining from sex strengthens communication skills as one's relationship is challenged to grow in verbal and emotional levels.

3. It allows time to develop a full understanding of love.

4. It allows time to develop close friendships with many people.

5. It avoids the guilt and anxiety associated with the fear of being pregnant, being "caught" when sexually involved, and with actually being pregnant.

6. It avoids the physical health risks previously discussed.

Reprinted with permission from *Love and Relationships: God's Plan for Human Sexuality*. Thomas and Donna Finn. Copyright 1991. Hi-Time Publishing Corp.

Appendix B

Resources for Further Readings

Writings of Pope John Paul II

Familiaris Consortio: The Role of the Christian Family in the Modern World. Boston: St. Paul Books & Media, 1981.

Original Unity of Man and Woman—Catechesis of the Book of Genesis. Boston: St. Paul Books & Media, 1980.

Reflections on Humanae Vitae. Boston: St. Paul Books & Media, 1984.

Writings of Pope Paul VI

Humanae Vitae: Of Human Life. Boston: St. Paul Books & Media, 1968.

Other Resources

Balsam, Charles and Elizabeth. *Family Planning—A Guide for Exploring the Issues.* Liguori, MO: Liguori Publications, 1986.

Finn, T. and Finn, D. *Love and Relationships: God's Plan for Human Sexuality.* Milwaukee: Hi-Time Publishing Corp., 1991.

Grace, M. and Grace, J. *A Joyful Meeting: Sexuality in Marriage.* St. Paul, MN: International Marriage Encounter, 1980.

Kippley, J. and Kippley, S. *The Art of Natural Family Planning*. Cincinnati: Couple to Couple League, 1984. (Most comprehensive discussion of NFP)

Kippley, J. *Sex and the Marriage Covenant—A Basis for Morality*. Cincinnati: Couple to Couple League, 1991.

Mast, C. K. *Love and Life: A Christian Sexual Morality Guide for Teens*. San Francisco: Ignatius Press, 1986.

Rousseau, M. and Gallagher, C. *Sex Is Holy*. Amity House, Inc., 1986.

Smith, J. E. *Humanae Vitae—A Generation Later*. Washington, D.C.: The Catholic University of America Press, 1991.

Thyma, P. *The Double Check Method of Family Planning*. Collegeville, MN: The Liturgical Press, 1978. (Sympto-Thermal method of NFP)

Wilson, M. A. *Love and Fertility*. BBE Publishers, 1986. (Ovulation method of NFP)

Notes

1. Second Vatican Council, *Pastoral Constitution on the Church in the Modern World* (Boston: St. Paul Books & Media, 1965): no. 16.

2. J. Kippley, *Sex and the Marriage Covenant* (Cincinnati: Couple to Couple League, 1991), 76-86.

3. L. Bumpas and J. Sweet, "National Estimates of Cohabitation," *Demography* 26 (1989): 615.

4. U.S. Bureau of Census, 1986.

5. J. Healy, *Cohabitation Policy Overview* (Diocese of Peoria, IL, Office of Family Life, November 1988).

6. N. Bennett, A. Blanc and D. Bloom, "Commitment and the Modern Union: Assessing the Link Between Pre-Marital Cohabitation and Subsequent Marital Stability," *American Sociological Review* 53 (1988): 127-138.

7. P. Blumstein and P. Schwartz, *American Couples: Money, Work and Sex* (New York: William Morrow, 1983).

8. Blumstein and Schwartz, *American Couples.*

9. Bennett, Blanc and Bloom, "Commitment and the Modern Union," 127-138.

10. J. Teachman and K. Paasch, "Legal Status and the Stability of Coresidential Unions," *Demography* 28 (1991): 571.

11. K. Tanfer, "Patterns of Pre-Marital Cohabitation Among Never Married Women in the U.S.," *Journal of Marriage and the Family* 49 (1987): 483-497.

12. Bumpas and Sweet, "Estimates of Cohabitation," 615.

13. Most Rev. J. Fiorenza, "Cohabitating Couples Who Seek Church Marriage," *Origins* 17 (1987): 431-432.

14. Pope John Paul II, *The Role of the Christian Family in the Modern World* (Boston: St. Paul Books & Media, 1981): no. 80.

15. Pope Paul VI, *Of Human Life* (Boston: St. Paul Books & Media, 1968): no. 14.

16. W. Mosher, "Contraceptive Practice in the United States, 1982-1988," *Family Planning Perspectives* 22 (1990): 198-205.

17. The Roper Organization, "1985 Virginia Slims American Women's Opinion Poll," Digest, *Family Planning Perspectives* 18 (1986): 36.

18. Kippley, *Marriage Covenant*. (See 309-322 for a discussion of the "Onan debate.")

19. Pope Sixtus V, *Effraenatum*, 1588.

20. Pope Paul VI, *Human Life*, no. 10.

21. Kippley, *Marriage Covenant*, 309-322.

22. Parke-Davis, Division of Warner-Lambert. Advertisement for Loestrin Low Estrogen Pill, appearing in *Family Planning Perspectives* 16 (January 1984).

23. Palan, *American Journal of Obstetrics and Gynecology* 161 (1989): 881.

24. Digest, *Family Planning Perspectives* 21 (1989): 190.

25. Data from University of North Carolina at Chapel Hill as published in the *Journal of the American Medical Association* 262 (December 8, 1989).

26. Data... *Journal of the American Medical Association* 262 (December 8, 1989).

27. J. Taylor, Journal of the American Academy of Dermatology, as cited in Med Watch, *Family Foundations*, (March–April, 1990): 3.

28. R. Noble, "There Is No Safe Sex," *Newsweek* (April 1, 1991): 8.

29. L. Rosenberg and C. Mettlin, American Journal of Epidemiology, December 1990, as cited in Med Watch, *Family Foundations*, (May–June 1991): 3.

30. Digest, *Family Planning Perspectives* 22 (1990): 238.

31. F. Frech, "Update on Teen Pregnancy," *Heartbeat Quarterly* (Summer, 1980).

32. J. Rosoff, President, Alan Guttmacher Institute, letter to AGI Associates, December 9, 1988.

33. E. Jones and D. Forrest, "Contraceptive Failure Rates Based on the 1988 NSFG," *Family Planning Perspectives* 24 (1992): 15-19.

34. P. Weckenbrock, "Evidence that Requires a Conclusion," *Family Foundations* (May–June, 1991): 19.

35. J. Little, "Naming Good and Evil," *First Things* 23 (1992): 23-30.

36. Pope John Paul II, *Christian Family*, no. 80.

37. G. K. Doring, and A. Socher, "Erfahrungen mit einer sympto-thermalen Methode zur Familien-planung," *Geburts u. Frauenbeilk* 48 (1988): 106-108, translated in *Family Foundations* (March–April, 1989): 1.

38. J. Trussel and L. Grummer-Straun, "Contraceptive Failure of the Ovulation Method of Periodic Abstinence," *Family Planning Perspectives* 22 (1990): 65-75.

39. L. Atkinson, R. Lincola and J. Forrest, "The Next Contraceptive Revolution," *Family Planning Perspectives* 18 (1986): 1.

40. W. Grady, et al. "Contraceptive Failure in the United States: Estimates," *Family Planning Perspectives* 18 (1986): 204.

41. "The Joy of Protected Sex," *McCall's Magazine* 118 (September 1990).

42. J. Ross, "Contraception: Short-term vs. Long-term Failure Rates," *Family Planning Perspectives* 21 (1989): 275-277.

43. Jones and Forrest, "Contraceptive Failure Rates," 15-19.

44. W. Miller, "Why Some Women Fail to Use Their Contraceptive Method: A Psychological Investigation," *Family Planning Perspectives* 18 (1986): 27-32.

45. Jones and Forrest, "Contraceptive Failure Rates," 15-19.

46. R. Fehring, D. Laurence, and C. Savage, "Self-Esteem, Spiritual Well-being and Intimacy: A Comparison Among Couples Using NFP and Oral Contraceptives," *International Review of Natural Family Planning/Human Life Issues* 13 (1989): 3-4.

47. N. Aguilar, *The New No-Pill, No-Risk Birth Control* (New York: Rawson Associates, 1986).

48. J. Kippley, "Finley Is in Dark on the True Nature of NFP," *Family Foundations* (May-June, 1991): 5.

49. Djerassi, C. as cited in Schwartz, J. "Rhythm Without Blues," *Discover* (March, 1991): 22.

St. Paul Book & Media Centers

ALASKA
750 West 5th Ave., Anchorage, AK 99501 907-272-8183.

CALIFORNIA
3908 Sepulveda Blvd., Culver City, CA 90230 310-397-8676.
1570 Fifth Ave. (at Cedar Street), San Diego, CA 92101 619-232-1442;
    619-232-1443.
46 Geary Street, San Francisco, CA 94108 415-781-5180.

FLORIDA
145 S.W. 107th Ave., Miami, FL 33174 305-559-6715; 305-559-6716.

HAWAII
1143 Bishop Street, Honolulu, HI 96813 808-521-2731.

ILLINOIS
172 North Michigan Ave., Chicago, IL 60601 312-346-4228; 312-346-3240.

LOUISIANA
4403 Veterans Memorial Blvd., Metairie, LA 70006 504-887-7631;
    504-887-0113.

MASSACHUSETTS
50 St. Paul's Ave., Jamaica Plain, Boston, MA 02130 617-522-8911.
Rte. 1, 885 Providence Hwy., Dedham, MA 02026 617-326-5385.

MISSOURI
9804 Watson Rd., St. Louis, MO 63126 314-965-3512; 314-965-3571.

NEW JERSEY
561 U.S. Route 1, Wick Plaza, Edison, NJ 08817 908-572-1200.

NEW YORK
150 East 52nd Street, New York, NY 10022 212-754-1110.
78 Fort Place, Staten Island, NY 10301 718-447-5071; 718-447-5086.

OHIO
2105 Ontario Street (at Prospect Ave.), Cleveland, OH 44115 216-621-9427.

PENNSYLVANIA
214 W. DeKalb Pike, King of Prussia, PA 19406 215-337-1882; 215-337-2077.

SOUTH CAROLINA
243 King Street, Charleston, SC 29401 803-577-0175.

TEXAS
114 Main Plaza, San Antonio, TX 78205 210-224-8101.

VIRGINIA
1025 King Street, Alexandria, VA 22314 703-549-3806.

CANADA
3022 Dufferin Street, Toronto, Ontario, Canada M6B 3T5 416-781-9131.